DEPRESSION
RELIEF
JOURNAL

Creative Prompts & Mindfulness
Practices to Release Negative Emotions

MAGGIE C. VAUGHAN, LMFT, PhD

Illustrations by Jacinta Kay

**ROCKRIDGE
PRESS**

For general information on our other products and services or to obtain technical support, please contact our Customer Care Department within the United States at (866) 744-2665, or outside the United States at (510) 253-0500.

Rockridge Press publishes its books in a variety of electronic and print formats. Some content that appears in print may not be available in electronic books, and vice versa.

Interior and Cover Designer: Amanda Kirk
Art Producer: Megan Baggott
Editor: Jed Bickman
Production Manager: Sandy Noman

Illustrations © 2021 Jacinta Kay
Author photo courtesy of New Moon Photography

Paperback ISBN: 978-1-63878-157-8
eBook ISBN: 978-1-63807-771-8
R0

Introduction

When I think back to the time I spent burdened by depression in my teens and twenties, it's like thinking about a different person. I feel sorry for that other "me" and wish she'd known of an established, direct route to contentment. Fortunately, via a circuitous and sometimes agonizing journey, that younger "me" did eventually emerge on the other side of depression, thanks in no small part to the aid of mindfulness.

I hadn't set out to pursue mindfulness, but rather unwittingly fell into it. At the age of 22, I moved to Los Angeles and, since the entire city was doing it, took up the practice of yoga. I was not a fan initially, but yoga grew on me, became an obsession, and was ultimately my lifesaver.

Yoga provided a sense of contentment, calm, and focus I previously lacked. I'll never forget the moment I had the realization that "I feel okay … I am okay … everything is okay." Through mindfulness, yoga taught me how to observe sensations and thoughts without reacting to them. With that mindfulness came hopeful and accepting ways of viewing myself and my world.

These experiences with mindfulness and depression inspired me to pursue graduate degrees in psychology and a career providing others with the type of support I once needed. Joining others in their journeys through depression has been exactly the honor I expected it would be. This journal is my effort to offer support, direction, and comfort to those outside my personal and professional circles who struggle with depression. It represents a collection of simple yet effective perspectives and exercises for transforming depression into hope. Please approach it with an open mind, at your own pace, and in your own way.

How to Use This Journal

This journal offers creative and practicable activities for overcoming depression through mindfulness. Feel free to engage with them in any order; it is not necessary to work sequentially. Since the practices in this journal vary in approach and focus, you might find yourself gravitating toward different activities from one day to the next, depending on how you feel and your present circumstances. If you're short on time or have a limited attention span, you might consider committing to just one exercise daily to sustain momentum and develop the habit of mindfulness without having to set aside large amounts of time.

There are four types of mindfulness practices contained here:

- Writing prompts

- Creative prompts

- Mindfulness-based practices

- Affirmations

Each form of practice takes a unique route to mindfulness. Writing allows us to externalize our inner experiences so we can more clearly, and literally, "see" them. Creative prompts provide a playful means to manifest tranquility and bring us into the present moment. Mindfulness-based practices include formal and informal mind-body exercises to bring awareness to our inner experiences so we can better understand and respond to ourselves and our life's stressors.

All the exercises will help you process and work through uncomfortable thoughts and feelings, facilitate a sense of connectedness to yourself and others, and foster clarity. Please try not to critique the outcomes of the exercises. The goal here is not to produce impressive pieces of writing or artwork; rather, it is simply to reach a nonjudgmental state of self-awareness.

Working through depression is a courageous, weighty, often uncomfortable process. As you become increasingly mindful, you might find yourself face-to-face with some unsettling thoughts and sensations. Give yourself permission to take breaks and move at your own pace, but please do not give up. Remember that discomfort is the best friend of progress.

This book is not intended as a substitute for professional help. If you're working with a mental health provider, please keep doing so. If you have thoughts of self-harm or symptoms lasting more than two weeks, or find that depression is interfering with your ability to function effectively at work, school, or in your relationships, please reach out to your primary care physician or a mental health professional. In addition, if any of the exercises contained here trigger acute discomfort, please consider doing them under the guidance of a licensed expert. For local mental health resources, see FindTreatment.SAMHSA.gov.

Decoding Depression

Depression is a common, treatable medical condition that affects one's ability to fully engage with and enjoy life. According to the National Alliance on Mental Illness, over 19 million adults in the United States, or about 8 percent of the population, have experienced one or more depressive episodes within the past year. Depression affects people of all ages, races, and genders.

Depression ranges from mild to severe and isn't always recognizable. Some experience its more notorious symptoms, such as sadness, hopelessness, or suicidal thoughts. Others, however, may simply suffer from one or more of depression's lesser-known symptoms, like chronic fatigue or low energy. In all cases, depression makes it challenging to feel fully able to live as one's best self.

Depression is not a character flaw, nor is it a sign of weakness. Depression doesn't need a reason, like trauma or loss. Sufferers cannot simply will themselves out of it. In fact, depression is a medical condition, affecting a person's biochemistry. The cause is complex, deriving from a variety of influences such as environmental factors, genetic predisposition, family and relational experiences, and personality. Fortunately, depression is one of the most treatable mental health conditions.

THE BODY

Depression is often mistaken as a purely emotional experience; however, depression can negatively affect the body as well. In fact, some individuals experience depression in a purely physical manner. The most common physical manifestations of depression are fatigue; difficulty sleeping or excess sleep; joint, limb, or back pain; vague aches; gastrointestinal problems; and appetite changes. Overeating and undereating are common and can lead to significant changes in weight. Due to fatigue and low energy, someone who is depressed might move or speak slowly and feel unmotivated to pursue activities they would otherwise enjoy. Considering all of this, it's no wonder people with depression feel unable to access and live as their true selves.

THOUGHTS AND BELIEFS

Depression is like a sieve through which what's possible and good gets filtered out, leaving a residue of all that is bad and not working. This negative cognitive filter impedes the depressed person's ability to see from a variety of perspectives, particularly positive ones. It becomes a challenge to envision options, which hampers one's ability to effectively problem-solve and misleads the depressed person into believing they're "stuck." The negative bias of depression also causes personal strengths to go unnoticed, leading to thoughts like "I am incapable" or "I am worthless." Tunnel vision can also lead to pessimism about the future and disillusionment in relationships. One study found that relative to nondepressed individuals, depressed patients recognized fewer positive aspects in their parents, significant others, and themselves, and identified a greater number of negative traits. Prolonged or severe depression can trigger thoughts of self-harm or suicide.

EMOTIONAL PATTERNS

Unlike sadness, which comes and goes in tandem with life's ups and downs, depression is a prolonged low mood that often has no known trigger. Depression often undermines social, recreational, and work enjoyment and functioning. Emotional symptoms listed among the criteria for a diagnosis of major depressive disorder by the *Diagnostic and Statistical Manual of Mental Disorders* (*DSM-5*) include "feeling sad or having a depressed mood," the loss of pleasure in previously enjoyed activities, and feelings of worthlessness or guilt. Mood symptoms range from mild to severe and need to last at least two weeks to be diagnosed.

Compared to nondepressed individuals, people with depression more frequently express negative emotions like fear, sadness, and resentment and less commonly convey positive experiences such as joy, affection, and enthusiasm. Depression also disrupts emotional regulation, causing excessive lethargy or disinterest among some, and irritability or volatility among others. An unstable mood can disable the social functions served by emotional regulation, like appropriate social engagement and the forming of cooperative and meaningful relationships. Unfortunately, some mistake their depressive mood as a reflection of a weak character, which worsens symptoms and creates a snowball effect of negative emotions.

The Power of Creativity, Journaling & Mindfulness

Mindful creativity, journaling, and meditative exercises direct our curiosity to the present moment, heightening attunement to our internal and external worlds. These moments of hyper-cognizance offer a respite from the ruminations of a mind that tends to dwell upon past regrets and worry about future unknowns. In this stillness, mindfulness allows us to fully experience and more clearly understand the significance of physical and emotional sensations, thoughts, and external circumstances. Increased awareness, in turn, provides us with insight into the most relevant aspects of our life and innermost needs. With this understanding, we increase our capacity to respond empathically and effectively to ourselves and to others, and in different circumstances. When practiced regularly, mindfulness actually leads to structural changes in the brain—changes that reinforce ongoing mindfulness, emotional regulation, self-awareness, and compassion.

CREATIVE PROMPTS

Creativity offers a safe and absorbing path to achieving mindfulness, relaxing us and preventing acute emotions from dominating our perception. It provides a playful means of getting close to our emotions without the threat of being swallowed by them. This level of protection promotes curiosity, exploration, and the symbolic expression of events and feelings that might normally be too distressing to confront. Creativity allows us to literally and symbolically manipulate the meaning and power we give our emotions and life stories, and frees us to consider new ways of seeing ourselves and our worlds. With control over our creativity, we feel empowered to make change and we gain satisfaction—even a measurable dopamine boost—from our accomplishments. By expressing and seeing ourselves through a creative lens, we shift our perspective to one of acceptance, connection, and possibility. All of the creative prompts in this book are designed to heighten mindfulness and a sense of calm.

WRITING PROMPTS

By putting our thoughts, feelings, and experiences into writing, we externalize our inner worlds and can view them more objectively. Writing activities
offer a pause from life's omnipresent distractions, clearing the way for us to
see and reflect upon our circumstances. Converting thoughts and feelings into
the written word can help us process and dampen painful emotions, helping
the brain transition out of fight-or-flight mode into a calmer state that's better
equipped to find solutions. Numerous studies have demonstrated the benefits
of expressive writing for mental and physical health. Just a few of the possible
benefits include:

- Lower blood pressure

- Improved immune function

- Elevated mood and feelings of well-being

- Decrease in post-traumatic and depressive symptoms

- Reduction in work absences

- Enhanced performance in school and sports

- Improvements in social behavior

MINDFULNESS

Mindfulness exercises encompass a variety of activities designed to help us
quiet our wandering minds and attain a state of nonjudgmental awareness of the
present moment. These practices can be formal, such as in meditation, or informal and easily undertaken during everyday activities. Unlike other approaches
to improving psychological well-being, mindfulness seeks to have us step into an
objective state of observing—as opposed to changing—our cognitive states. When
we discover we can sit with uncomfortable thoughts and feelings, their grip upon
us weakens.

The practice of mindfulness begets a mindful life. When we're mindful, we
suffer less, as we can better self-regulate in the face of life's ups and downs. We
recognize discomfort but are not manipulated by it, and we can more readily see
meaning and find enjoyment in life's minutiae. Studies have shown the benefits
of mindfulness-based practices in reducing and treating depressive symptoms.

♡

I embrace every aspect of who
I am, as they are all
human and deserving of love.

FANCY TREE EXERCISE FOR FOSTERING AWARENESS

Decorate the trees below to demonstrate their unique differences in texture, color, shape, leaves, and branches.

Example

Re-experiencing a Positive Moment

What we imagine, we feel. Use this exercise to relive a positive moment.

Think of a positive experience you had within the past day or two. Take a few minutes to list every detail you can recall about that event. What did you see, hear, smell, taste? How did you feel emotionally? Physically? What made this occurrence enjoyable or meaningful to you?

_____

_____

_____

_____

_____

_____

_____

_____

_____

_____

_____

_____

_____

SMALL ME, WISE ME

The images below represent two parts of you: *small you* (the vulnerable inner child that lives in all of us) and *wise you*. Fill in *small you*'s dialogue bubble with thoughts that keep you stuck. Use *wise you*'s dialogue bubble to help *small you* shift their perspective and get unstuck.

Setting a Daily Intention

Taking a few minutes in the morning to set a daily intention can significantly affect your entire day. An intention reflects an internal attitude or orientation, such as curiosity or compassion, that you'd like to guide you through your day.

Begin by taking a few slow breaths, making sure to fully exhale. Once you feel relaxed, consider the following:

- What matters most to me today?

- How would I like to experience my day?

- What would make today meaningful to me?

- What one attitude would help me foster compassion toward myself today?

- What intention would help me foster compassion toward others?

- What intention would allow me to feel most connected to the natural world?

- What intention would best provide comfort to me today?

Once you've chosen your intention for the day, write it down, say it out loud, and keep it nearby as a reminder. It could be as simple as, *Today I will stay in the present moment.*

LINE GRAPH FOR BREATH AWARENESS

Breathe in and out slowly and naturally. Visualize your breath coming and going. Record what you see on the graph.

Now, tense up your shoulders. Observe, visualize, and record your breathing.

How did tensing up affect your breathing?

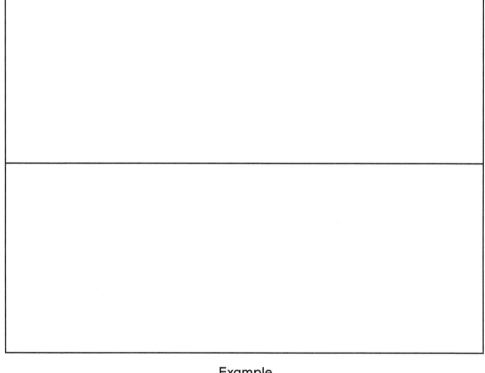

Example

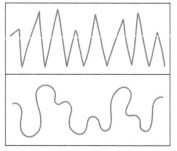

Living Authentically

If you were to live as your truest version of yourself, in keeping with what you most enjoy doing and what you like most about yourself, what would be different? What keeps you from pursuing this way of life? If you were to live in this way, what relationships would be threatened? What fears arise when you imagine living in this way?

DRAWING BUBBLE BREATH

We're often told to "take a deep breath," when in fact relaxation occurs when we fully exhale. Here, we'll create long exhales in order to relax.

Breathe slowly. Without force, fully release your breath as you exhale. Now, visualize each exhale in the shape of a bubble. Can you create 10 bubbles of different shapes? Draw your bubbles below.

Lotus Flower Exercise: Bringing Awareness to How You Spend Your Time

Each lotus petal below represents one area of life. On the appropriate petal, jot down behaviors you engage in when you're feeling satisfied in the given area. Feel free to list the same behavior in more than one area.

Next, color in each layer to represent how fulfilled you are in the given area. Did you list any behaviors you could engage in more regularly?

Example

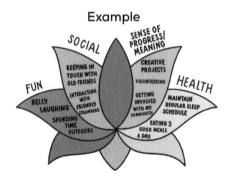

♡

I consciously take in
all the comforts
the world has to offer.

Knowing Your Triggers

We are all prone to behaving reactively under certain circumstances. When triggered, we tend to act instantaneously and without thought. When you know your triggers, you can plan for them and decide in advance how you would like to respond.

On the diagram below, label your triggers and unwanted responses, then identify alternative, more constructive responses.

Trigger	
Unwanted Response	
More Constructive Response	

Trigger	
Unwanted Response	
More Constructive Response	

Trigger	
Unwanted Response	
More Constructive Response	

Trigger	
Unwanted Response	
More Constructive Response	

LINE, LIGHT, AND TEXTURE DRAWING

Select any nearby object as your subject. First, draw only the lines you see around and within the object. Next, observe only the differing amounts of light upon and within the object and shade in your object accordingly. Now, see if you can use pressure, shading, or lines to represent texture. The goal here is to foster mindfulness by narrowing focus, and to practice observing in detail.

If You Were an Animal

Use this playful calming meditation to deepen insight into internal conflicts, concerns, or undiscovered parts of yourself.

Sitting or lying down, close your eyes and begin to breathe rhythmically. Inhale to the count of 4, hold your breath for 4 seconds, then release the breath completely to the count of 8. As you do this, give yourself permission to let go of physical tension and external concerns.

Once you're fully relaxed, continue breathing rhythmically and allow the image of your animal self to form. When an image surfaces, take some time to explore it. Notice its unique features, expressions, and movements. Consider whether this creature might represent known or unknown parts of yourself or internal conflicts, or if it serves a purpose.

FINDING THE LOST PARTS OF YOURSELF

Sometimes we bury some of the most enjoyable and interesting aspects of ourselves to avoid others' judgment and disappointment. In the space below, list the places (or moments) when you broke off a part of yourself. Consider what would happen if you brought them back and embraced them.

Shifting Your Perspective on Stress

Stress is not the result of what's happening around you; it's generated by the *meaning* your brain attaches to what's happening around you. Think about one aspect of your life that you find stressful or overwhelming. Is there a way to interpret it differently?

SELF-AWARENESS SCRIBBLE

Place the point of your writing utensil anywhere on the page. Scribble for 30 seconds without stopping. Don't move to the next step until you are done scribbling.

Notice how much of the page your scribble consumes. Are your lines wavy or sharp? How much pressure was used? What does your scribble say about you?

CONNECTING TO NATURE

Research shows that developing a strong connection to nature is linked to higher levels of emotional balance.

As you color in the pictures below, consider the many ways nature brings joy into your life. Can you think of ways you could engage with the natural world more regularly?

Loosening Your Dependencies

When we bind our happiness to specific people, outcomes, or conditions, our sense of well-being becomes dependent upon things out of our control, which can cause feelings of helplessness, depression, and angst.

What are the perceived "needs" in your life that you can begin viewing as "desires" or "preferences"?

♡

Resistance to hard work is normal.
I pursue my goals even when
a part of me wants to quit.

CULTIVATING COMPASSION TO
REDUCE SHARED SUFFERING

Think of someone in your life who is struggling. Draw an image below to represent that person.

Draw a heart around this "being" in a color that represents a sentiment, such as comfort, that you'd like to transmit to this person. Now, draw a second heart around this person in a color that symbolizes another sentiment. Continue to wrap this individual in colored hearts that represent all the feelings you'd like to send their way.

Full-Body Emotion Infusion

In a quiet, clutter-free environment, lie on your back or sit comfortably with your legs and arms uncrossed. Make sure you feel fully supported.

Choose one positive emotion, such as joy, that you'd like to experience.

Close your eyes.

Without judgment, as you breathe in slowly, try to visualize your chosen emotion in written form. Don't worry if you can't see every letter. (If you prefer, you may choose an object or color that represents your emotion instead.)

Hold on to the inhale until you can see your word.

Exhale very slowly. As you do, channel your emotion into any areas of your body that are experiencing tension. Notice your body letting go.

At the end of your exhale, breathe in your emotion again. Inhale until you can see it, then exhale as you release the emotion slowly while visualizing it spreading farther into your body. Notice how relaxed each body part becomes as it is infused with your selected emotion.

Continue until all desired parts of your body have been addressed, or as long as you wish.

Creating Your Safe Space

Imagine looking out your window and seeing the most soothing view possible. Can you draw a sketch of what you'd see? Bring this image to mind whenever you need a moment of calm.

Recipe for Happiness

Feeling content requires us to regularly prioritize healthy and rewarding habits, such as getting to bed at a certain time, routine exercise, and positive social engagements. Create an ingredient list for happiness that includes behaviors and activities you have found to nourish your mind, body, and soul.

EXTERNALIZING DISCOMFORT

Take a moment to identify a sensation of discomfort you are currently feeling. Close your eyes, and as you breathe rhythmically, focus completely on that sensation. When your mind wanders, gently redirect it. With curiosity, explore the discomfort. Does it have a shape? A color? Is it stagnant, or does it wander? What type of texture does it have? Once you have captured a detailed image, draw it below.

Quilting for Comfort

Historically, quilts have been made to provide both physical and emotional comfort. Add designs and/or color to create your own comforting quilt.

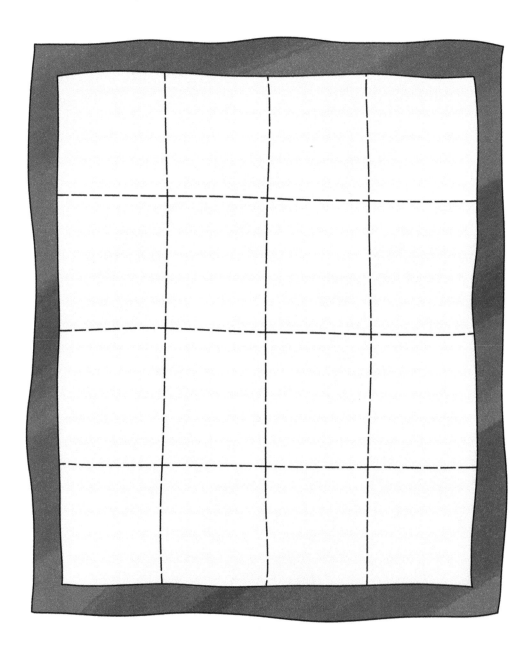

Shifting Your Reference Point to Improve Self-Worth

There's only one person in your life you should ever compare yourself to: you.

When we compare ourselves to others, we reduce our worth to one trait, such as intelligence or beauty, and lose sight of the full picture of who we are.

Take a moment to turn inward. Ask yourself:

How closely am I living in accordance with what matters most to me?

Are there any areas of my life in which I've gotten off track?

What am I most proud of about who I am and how I live my life?

♡

*I impart warmth to other
living things whenever possible.*

MOODY KITTY

Using only the shapes here, rearrange the cat in new positions to reflect its many moods.

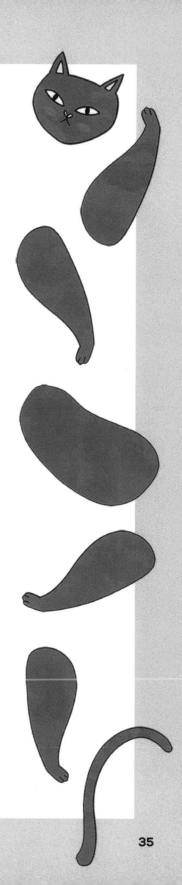

Example

Discovering Your Safe Space

Find a comfortable, quiet place to sit or lie on your back. Rest your arms on your legs if sitting, or along your sides if lying down. Make sure your legs are uncrossed.

Close your eyes.

Breathe in slowly, hold at the top of your inhale, then exhale slowly. Do this 10 times, while noticing your body becoming increasingly relaxed.

Imagine walking down a staircase while holding on to the railing. With each step, you sink deeper into a state of calm.

Notice as you descend that it leads to the most beautiful and comforting place you've ever seen. Take in the sights, sounds, smells, and temperature.

Now, take some time to explore this setting in greater detail. Recognize that it has everything you need to feel completely comforted and secure. You might be surprised by what you discover.

Stay here as long as you like, and remember that you can return to your safe space any time you need it.

NEVER-ENDING RAINBOW

Use this exercise to improve focus and reduce tension and stress.

Draw several parallel curves under the rainbow curve below. See how many curves you can fit on the page and try to shade each arc differently.

Example

Example

Three Things You're Grateful For

Our minds get caught in habitual ways of interpreting events and circumstances. By regularly listing things we are grateful for, we help build an adaptive habit of seeing from a positive perspective.

At the end of your day, list three specific things you felt grateful for today (for example, "the chocolate cake Mom made" rather than "food").

_____

_____

_____

_____

_____

_____

_____

_____

_____

If you do this regularly, list new items each time.

Antidote Exercise

The mind cannot experience two opposing emotions simultaneously. Choose colors to represent the destructive emotions listed on the left, as well as their antidotes listed on the right.

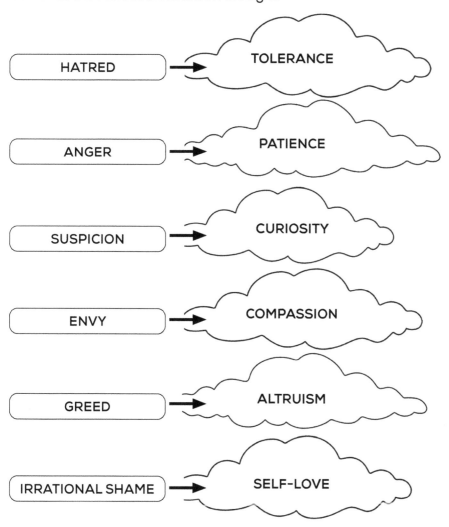

Moving forward, when a destructive emotion arises, see if you can imagine yourself enveloped in a colorful, soothing cloud that represents the needed antidote.

Facial Expression Exercise

This exercise will shed light on your interpersonal expectations and facilitate mindful engagement with others.

Circle the facial expressions below that reflect how you expect others to typically respond to you.

With an open mind and in a neutral manner, take a day to be particularly observant of how others engage with you.

Put a box around the faces that reflect your experience.

How accurately do your expectations match how others behave?

♡

I am quick to comfort my inner child, particularly when she is at her ugliest, as I know that acceptance brings her immediate calm.

Finding Meaning

Research indicates that having a sense of purpose in life contributes to contentedness, but did you know it also boosts immunity? Your purpose might come from one or many intentions and can be grand (such as ending poverty) or minor in scale (such as brightening the lives of others by expressing warmth).

• What are some ways you can pursue your purpose?

_____

_____

_____

_____

_____

_____

• How can you live out your purpose in everyday life?

_____

_____

_____

_____

_____

_____

_____

FACE LINE DRAWING

Without lifting your drawing utensil from the page, draw your face with one continuous line. Include all facial features.

Example

Body Scan

Body scan exercises provide a simple means to connect the mind and body, ground yourself, and consciously release physical tension.

Begin by sitting in a chair with your back upright, but not rigid. Plant your feet firmly on the ground, and rest your hands on top of your legs.

Inhale slowly and evenly through your nose, and exhale through your nose or mouth. Continue with this breathing method throughout this exercise.

Focus on your toes, soles, and ankles. Release any tension you have in those areas. Move to your calves and thighs, letting go of any tension you notice there. Next, fully relax your hips and buttocks. Now, free your lower, middle, and upper back of all unnecessary strain. Allow your shoulders, arms, wrists, and hands to fully relax. Give your neck and jaw permission to rest. Finally, release any stress you feel in your face and head.

Take a moment to recognize and enjoy your ability to significantly reduce your body's tension.

Viewing Your Thoughts as Clouds

Like clouds, our thoughts come and go. Observe your thoughts and record them in the clouds below. Imagine the clouds forming and vaporizing, just as our thoughts do.

Inserting a Pause

When we're threatened, our fight-or-flight response can trigger intense emotion and prompt us to react instantaneously. It may save our life, but it can also make us do things we deeply regret.

Remembering to pause after a trigger can be tremendously useful in preventing regrettable reactions.

Make a list of situations that you find triggering. What behaviors, such as deep breathing or taking a walk, might help you pause when triggered? List these, too.

LADDER EXERCISE: BECOMING PROCESS-ORIENTED

When we focus on the process of reaching goals, rather than the goals themselves, we reduce anxiety and avoidance, and increase pleasure.

On the rungs of the first ladder, record five major behaviors needed to reach a goal of yours, in order from bottom to top. These are actions you will take.

On the top rung of the next ladder, write down the first major step from the bottom of the ladder on the left. Below that, record two smaller actions you can immediately make toward reaching the top rung of the second ladder.

Feel free to use this ladder exercise to establish subsequent steps and set goals in any area.

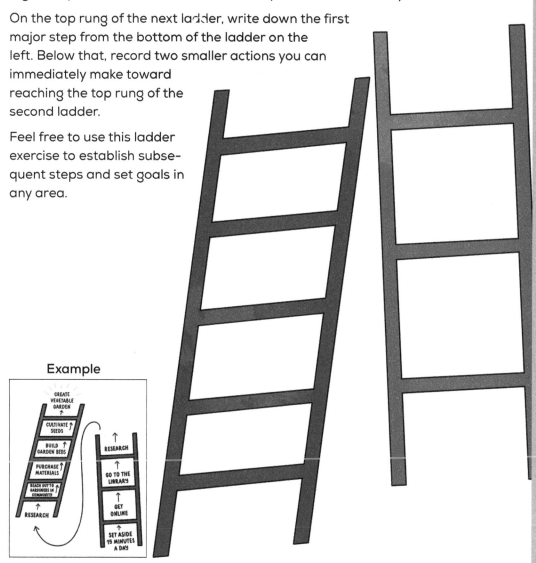

Example

CREATE VEGETABLE GARDEN
↑
CULTIVATE SEEDS ↑
BUILD GARDEN BEDS ↑
PURCHASE MATERIALS ↑
REACH OUT TO GARDENERS IN COMMUNITY ↑
↑
RESEARCH

↑
RESEARCH
↑
GO TO THE LIBRARY
↑
GET ONLINE
↑
SET ASIDE 15 MINUTES A DAY

MINDFUL DOODLE ACTIVITY

Select a shape or line segment. Draw the chosen shape or line repeatedly for a few minutes. Draw your images however you like—they might overlap, align, be of the same or differing sizes or orientations, or consist of one or more colors. As you do this, notice the feeling of your drawing utensil in your hand. Observe the feeling of changing the amount of pressure used as you draw. If you chose to use more than one color, see whether and how your mood shifts with the color change.

Why do you think you chose this line or shape?

♡

*I am not my thoughts.
I observe my thoughts with
curiosity and acceptance.*

Your Weekly Routine: Setting Boundaries

Being deliberate about how you spend your time elevates task efficiency and life enjoyment, and wards off burnout. The key to this is to set distinct boundaries between your workday and personal time, as well as between the workweek and weekend.

Write out your typical weekly routine.

_____

_____

_____

_____

_____

_____

_____

_____

_____

_____

_____

Review your routine. How clear are the divisions between work and playtime?

ANIMAL FOLLY

Get creative and kindle a little joy by filling in the animals below with absurd colors and patterns. Consider using stripes, spots, symbols, and other designs.

Balloon Breath for Insomnia

Mindfulness is shown to treat insomnia and improve sleep quality. You can use this technique to induce relaxation and obtain some of sleep's benefits, even while awake.

First, set your intention on prioritizing relaxation, not sleep. When your mind wanders to the subject of sleep, redirect your attention to your breath and comfort.

On your bed, lie on your back with your legs uncrossed and arms by your sides. Make sure you are cool or warm, not hot. Quickly scan your body to ensure you are not tensing any muscles. Allow your body to sink heavily into your mattress.

Close your eyes and breathe in calmly and slowly through your nose. Hold for three seconds, then exhale fully through your mouth. As you exhale, gently blow out so that your breath makes a sound.

Repeat, but now as you exhale, envision a balloon being created by the air leaving your mouth. Each time you exhale, "see" a new balloon forming. Continue as long as you can, focusing on the balloon images and your tension-free body.

BLIND CONTOUR DRAWING FOR CENTERING

Hold up your nondominant hand so you can see it easily. Without looking down at the page, draw what you see, including all lines. Looking at the non-dominant hand rather than what is being drawn will generate a deep level of focus and mindfulness.

Celebrating Process vs. Outcome

When it comes to goals, investing in the process rather than focusing on the results helps us sustain interest and motivation and makes for a more satisfying day-to-day life.

Think about a major goal of yours. What motivates you to work toward it?

_____

_____

_____

List some internal factors, like a sense of accomplishment or learning, that you can cultivate to boost enjoyment in the process and keep you motivated.

_____

_____

_____

If you tend to be results-oriented, note one or two day-to-day rewards of moving toward this goal.

_____

_____

_____

"I SCREAM" FOR HAPPINESS

Build an elaborate ice cream sundae. Use all or some of the ingredients here, and feel free to add your own!

Losing Yourself

Spending time in a maze can help focus and calm the mind without causing fatigue. To make the most of this exercise, move deliberately, rather than rushing to finish.

Pain into Power

Whether it is heartbreak, rejection, neglect, trauma, or loss, pain is something we all experience. Painful experiences can make us question ourselves and our lives. Fortunately, over time, painful experiences can also bring about tremendous strength and insight. The purpose of this exercise is to assist you in converting your pain into power.

Take a moment to think about a painful experience. Consider:

What sources of support, such as a person or book, helped me through it?

What did I learn from the experience that could guide my decision-making moving forward?

What perspective(s) did this experience help me shift?

If I choose to, how might I use what I learned from this experience to improve the lives of others?

What did this experience teach me about something I'd like to have more of in my life?

What did this experience show me I don't want in my life?

Feel free to write your answers on a separate piece of paper.

♡

I love and accept others unconditionally,
particularly those who are unkind,
as I know they are the most wounded.

SQUIDOODLE

See if you can draw faces on the squid below to tell a story. Can you tell two very different stories using facial expressions?

Protective Triangle Meditation

This protective triangle exercise soothes feelings of vulnerability and sadness.

In a safe, comforting location, sit up straight in a cross-legged position on the floor or ground. If you are unable to sit on the ground, feel free to sit on a chair or bed. Rest your hands on your thighs.

Close your eyes. Inhale slowly through your nose. Hold your breath briefly, then exhale completely through your nose or mouth. Continue with five more cycles of breath, allowing yourself to become more relaxed.

After the fifth cycle, turn your attention upward. Begin to experience a sense of nurturance and warmth as you visualize a bright, triangular ray of light descending upon you. The light may be in the color of your choice.

Allow the light to fully encompass you. Take in its offer of protection, support, and encouragement as you continue breathing evenly.

Breathe in support and reassurance; breathe out tension. Feel yourself becoming increasingly encouraged, calm, and self-confident with each breath cycle.

CREATING A COLLAGE FOR SOMEONE YOU LOVE

Feeling socially connected is associated with lower levels of anxiety and depression, and higher levels of empathy and self-worth. To enhance your sense of connection to a loved one, draw or write in collage items that represent their special qualities and the feelings you have toward them.

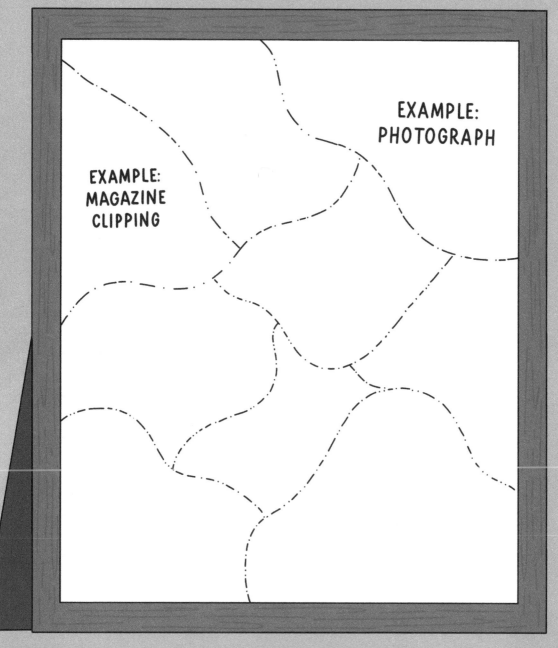

Web of Support

Social connectedness plays a significant role in happiness, health, and longevity. Even when we feel like being alone, we fare better when we socialize.

Sources of connection are not always obvious. They might include the "regulars" at our local coffee shop, our pets, and past relationships that have become dormant.

Make a list of your web of social connections. Include those you are closest to, but also write down sources of untapped or underappreciated connection.

....

....

....

....

....

How can you facilitate more routine or deeper levels of engagement with these connections?

....

....

....

....

....

....

SLOW WAVE DRAWING FOR LOWERING BLOOD PRESSURE AND HEART RATE

Beneath the sunset and island below, draw in several types of waves. When you draw a wave from left to right, try drawing it from right to left as well. Notice what it feels like to change direction and to make waves of differing shapes.

NUMBERS INTO CREATURES

Tap into your inner child to generate joy and boost cognitive flexibility and creativity.

Using the lines that form the numbers below as a starting point, draw a variety of objects or creatures.

8 6

2 5

Example

Seeing in Shades of Gray

When we evaluate ourselves, others, and situations and judge them as either all good or all bad, we contribute to emotional extremes and reactive behavior. This kind of thinking can also undermine positive habits when we conclude that we have failed rather than experienced a mere setback.

On the left, write any black-or-white evaluations you have of yourself, others, or circumstances. Next to them, write out alternative, less extreme interpretations.

How do these shifts in perspective affect your outlook?

Black-or-White Thoughts	Alternative Interpretations

♡

I can disappoint and
be disliked by others, and still
know that I am enough.

STILLNESS IN THE STORM

You don't have to absorb the chaos around you. In fact, remaining centered allows you to be more helpful and effective to others and yourself. Color in the circle at the center of this picture to represent yourself in a very calm state, then color in the storm around you.

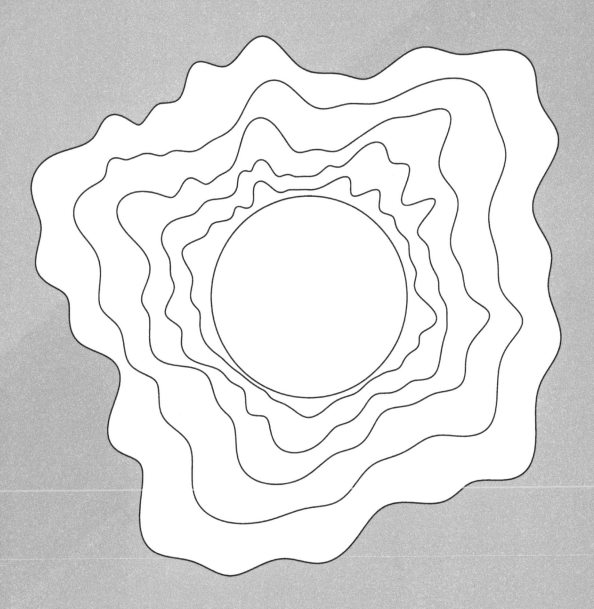

Bringing Mindfulness into Your Daily Routine

Select a routine activity, like brushing your teeth.

As you begin the activity, observe the thoughts entering and leaving your mind. Notice any physical sensations in your body. Bring awareness to your breath. Make note of any emotional sensations you are experiencing.

Move through every step of your activity with full awareness. As your mind wanders, gently guide it back to your activity. Notice how you experience the activity through each of your senses. What do you smell, feel, taste, hear, and see?

Once you complete your activity, ask yourself how fully engaging in the activity differed from being on autopilot. How many details can you recall from the activity? Did you discover anything new? How did you feel while doing the activity?

MEDITATIVE INFINITY SIGN TRACING

Slowly and deliberately follow the tracks to make multiple infinity signs. Try to stay within the lines that have been provided. Do this with your dominant as well as your nondominant hand. Begin each sign at a different starting point.

Example

Identifying Outdated Love-Seeking Habits

As young children, we seek out affection from our caregivers by learning and doing things they like. As adults, many of us continue to engage in the same love- and approval-seeking behaviors, even when they stop serving us and our relationships. Fill in the blanks in the following sentences:

When I was a kid, the person I wanted to feel most loved by was ....

This person was happiest with me when I .... , and when I did not ....

In my current relationships, this approval-seeking behavior may appear as ....

FLAG EXERCISE

Flags are often used to represent identity. Create a flag that reflects your unique self. Take into consideration your unique traits, talents, values, and interests.

Example

LETTING GO AND HOLDING ON TIME LINE

Above the following time line, note aspects of life you wish to hold on to. Beneath the line, record what you would like to leave behind. These can be activities, habits, rituals, behaviors, or something else.

Example

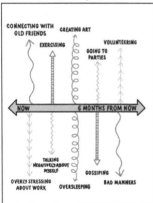

Space Exploration

This is a playful yet relaxing meditation for anytime you feel in need of a journey.

Start by lying on your back with legs outstretched and arms by your sides. Close your eyes. As you breathe in, think *relax*. Hold at the top of your inhale, then release, thinking *let go*. Carry on breathing in this manner for 10 full breath cycles.

Observe what you see with your eyes closed. Can you experience yourself moving through space in flickering darkness?

As you take in the vastness of space, see if you can relax your body so much that it feels weightless. Perhaps you can experience the sensation of floating in a gravity-free environment.

Take in the entirety of your journey through space. Enjoy how wonderful it feels to completely let go and float.

RAYS OF GRATITUDE

As you color in each of the sun's rays below, write in or think of one thing for which you are grateful.

♡

Self-doubt, sadness, and fear
might come along for the ride,
but they will not be driving.

Your Wandering Mind

Our minds wander about 50 percent of the time, and a wandering mind negatively affects mood. A focused mind, on the other hand, tends to be happy. List several activities you routinely engage in over the course of a month, such as going on a walk or hanging out with friends. Highlight the ones you find most satisfying. Now, circle the ones you find the most absorbing. Do you see a correlation?

PIN THE CROWN ON THE ROOSTER

The most distinctive feature on a rooster is his comb, or crown. For a spike in mood and problem-solving ability, give each rooster a unique crown.

Example

SELF-LOVE STICKY NOTES

Provide yourself with some self-support by writing self-care reminders,
personal mantras, and favorite quotes on the sticky notes.
Feel free to create some to hang around your home and workspace.

Thoughts on Butterflies

When done regularly, this exercise will help you note intrusive thoughts and unwanted emotions without feeling disturbed by them or compelled to react.

In a safe and comfortable location free of distractions, sit on a chair, or sit cross-legged on the ground.

Gently close your eyes. Take a deep, cleansing breath, hold it in for just a moment, and then let it go. Repeat 3 times, allowing yourself to sink into a peaceful state of relaxation.

Begin to observe your thoughts as they enter your mind. Just notice them, as you would watch butterflies fluttering around you. Simply see them coming and going, coming and going, separate from you.

Do this for several minutes, noticing how still and calm you can remain as various thoughts enter, then leave.

MANDALA COLORING FOR LOWERING ANXIETY

Multiple studies show that coloring mandalas significantly lowers anxiety. Color in the mandala below to help you unwind.

Labeling Depression in Your Body

Name the physical sensations you experience in your body when you're feeling depressed. Add color to the body and labels to represent each sensation.

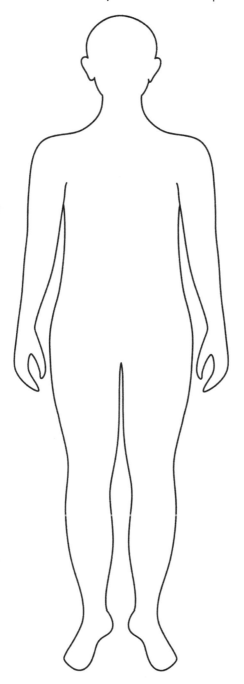

Laughter

Laughter offers an easy and affordable means of reducing stress hormones and lowering anxiety and depression.

What are the regular sources of humor in your life? In what situations are you most likely to laugh?

Make a list of activities, people, and situations that make you laugh.

BOOK COVER: TAKING CONTROL OF YOUR NARRATIVE

Create an autobiographical book cover that sums up your life as a story of resilience, courage, or triumph over adversity.

Stranger on a Foreign Planet

During an outdoor stroll, imagine that you have arrived from outer space and have never experienced anything like your current surroundings.

As you walk, take in the detail of the objects around you. If your mind wanders, gently guide it back to your new environment.

Notice the height, width, shape, and texture of trees. Observe the movement of grass, plants, and any creatures you pass. How do you experience these things now that you are taking them in as if for the first time? If you come across animals or people, what is your understanding of their behavior?

Give a new name to the objects you see without putting much thought into the names you choose. State these names aloud and listen closely to your voice as you speak. How do your voice and these new words sound to you?

♡

I am strong.
I am courageous.
I set fear aside and
move forward anyway.

COURAGEOUS LION

It takes courage to face life's challenges when depressed. On each large tuft of the lion's mane, list the strengths or coping skills that have helped you through tough times. On the smaller tufts, list strengths or coping skills that you're working on or hope to develop.

Your Wants and Needs Matter, Too

At times, it feels risky to assert our wants and needs, especially when we are eager to gain acceptance or avoid criticism. As a result, we sometimes make decisions based on what others want, which can lead to resentment and depression if done habitually.

Who is it you most often make decisions for?

....

....

....

What fears do you have about asserting your wants and needs?

....

....

....

Celebrating Individuality

Everyone is unique, and that's as it should be. On each of the stems below, create a different plant. Feel free to get silly!

EASY, FUN CUBIST PROCESS ART

Draw a simple version of an object, such as a flower, dog, or hand. Draw several curved lines diagonally across the page. Draw a different pattern in each section and then color it in.

Apology Letter

Think of a time when you hurt someone. Compose a letter explaining what contributed to your behavior. Take ownership of your mistake and the pain you caused, and note how you have grown since making it. Apologize. This is not a note to send; it's to help understand and work through a past mistake. Finally, forgive yourself and acknowledge your humanness and growth since that time.

DECORATIVE DOODLE FOR RELAXATION

Research suggests that doodling activates the brain's reward pathways and helps regulate mood.

This doodle can be done in one or several sittings.

Begin by drawing one curved line that crosses itself several times and expands to all sides of the page. Fill in each of the spaces you've created with designs, color blocks, or images.

Example

Where Do You Store Your Pain?

Most of us have one particularly vulnerable spot in the body where unprocessed emotions get stored. The most common areas are the intestines, shoulders and neck, lower back, and head. When symptoms such as aches or tension occur regularly, it's important to consider what causes them and whether such triggers can be addressed.

In a quiet space, lie on your back, with legs uncrossed and arms at your sides. Close your eyes. Inhale to a count of four, hold to a count of two, and exhale to a count of eight. Do this three times, deeply relaxing with each exhale.

Now, draw your attention to where you presently feel discomfort. Explore the sensations you feel. Ask yourself what your pain might represent. Could it be an emotion? Could it be a traumatic or upsetting experience?

If possible, place a hand over your pain. When you inhale, think *love*, and as you exhale, think *support*. Repeat 10 times, each time sending love and support to the area.

♡

I feel anger, but it is separate from me.
I can choose not to engage with it.
I will give anger the time
and space it needs to go away.

STILLNESS IN LIFE

Color or shade in the still life below. Take your time and try to breathe slowly and evenly throughout this exercise.

Your Unwinding Routine

Adequate sleep is crucial for physical and mental well-being. An unwinding bedtime ritual can be a useful means of enabling comforting rest. This ritual should include time for your mind and body to transition from an active mode to a relaxed state, through calming activities in a tranquil atmosphere.

What activities, like reading or listening to music, help you relax?

....

....

....

What are the elements of a tranquil sleep environment for you?

....

....

....

KANDINSKY-INSPIRED CIRCLES

Draw three concentric, imperfect circles of different sizes within each box. Then, fill each square with a unique combination of colors.

Example

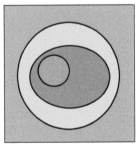

All about Me Thumbprint

In one constant stream of thought, fill in the lines of the thumbprint below to reflect your sense of self. Pay no attention to grammar or flow.

Honest Letter of Support

Take a few minutes to write a letter to yourself. List and thank yourself for the ways in which you take care of yourself. Then, write out some suggestions for better supporting yourself. Provide some encouragement and faith in your ability to provide such support.

Dear .... ,

_____

_____

_____

_____

_____

_____

_____

_____

_____

_____

_____

_____

_____

_____

FEATHER DRAWINGS

The repetitive strokes involved in drawing feathers have a soothing, centering effect. On the stems below, create different feathers, paying particular attention to lines and shading.

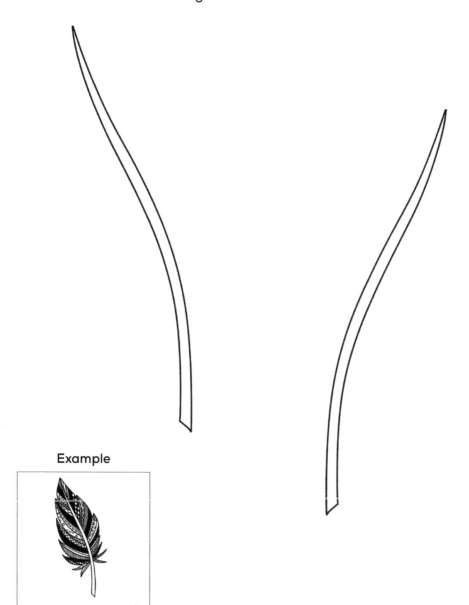

Example

Connecting with Nature

Mindful nature walks elevate well-being, focus, and immunity while reducing feelings of isolation.

Select a pleasant outdoor location to go on a walk and set your intention to connect with nature through each of your senses.

Notice the colors, textures, shapes, and movement in what you see. Observe the feeling of the air on your skin. Is it moist or dry? Still or moving? Become aware of all that you hear. How many distinct sounds can you identify? Observe your environment through your sense of smell. What do you detect?

Take a moment to recognize the aspects of nature you appreciate most. Ask yourself how nature enhances your life. Either aloud or to yourself, express your gratitude to the natural world for its offerings.

Creating Color Palettes

On the painter's palettes, create different color groupings. Notice which combination you enjoy most. See if you can generate or represent various emotional states by combining different colors.

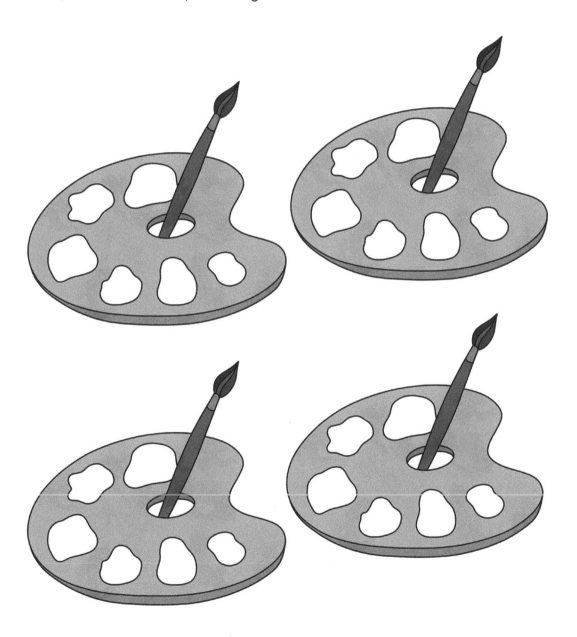

♡

*I live in accordance with what
I know to be true, and I do not try
to predict future unknowns.*

Your Core Self

Life's demands, others' expectations, and our own perfectionism can lead us down paths that do not align with our authentic selves. How well do you know your core self?

As a child, what did you want to do when you grew up?

....

....

....

Which of your personality traits do you enjoy most?

....

....

....

Whose approval, if anyone's, do you strive for? Is it your own or someone else's?

....

....

....

When are you most content?

....

....

....

MEDITATIVE LINE, CIRCLE, AND DOT CONSTELLATIONS

This activity promotes open-mindedness and calm. As you do this activity, focus on each mark as you make it, without an overall plan.

Begin by creating a constellation of closed shapes, such as circles, ovals, or teardrops. Extending out from the cluster, draw straight or curved lines. The lines may be dotted or solid. Finally, add some dots around your constellation.

Repeat until the page is covered.

Example

RAIN FOREST DETAIL

Create and immerse yourself in another world! Add density and biodiversity to the rain forest below by drawing in vines, plants, trees, flowers, and varied jungle creatures. Consider the manner in which you are sketching and the content of your drawing. What does it seem to be saying?

Mindfulness Practice for Reducing Judgment

Emotions can obstruct our ability to see broadly. As a result, we often make snap judgments about the behaviors of ourselves and others.

Mindfulness allows us to consider other possible interpretations, facilitating understanding and acceptance.

What is a judgment you've made about yourself or someone else? How many other ways could you explain your/their behavior?

EXPRESSING YOURSELF

When you are attuned to your emotional state, you're able to respond to it with greater compassion and efficacy. Draw lines that reflect each of the emotions named below.

SURPRISED   CHEERFUL   LONELY

ASHAMED   ANGRY   GUILTY

WORRIED   EAGER   PROUD

INTIMIDATED   AMUSED   OPTIMISTIC

PEACEFUL   DISGUSTED   SELF-CONSCIOUS

CURIOUS   INADEQUATE   LOVING

Mindful Letter for Self-Compassion

Self-compassion refers to approaching ourselves with the same kindness and acceptance we would a friend. Rather than personalizing shortcomings, self-compassionate individuals know that having flaws is a universal human experience, which provides an effective buffer against shame, doubt, self-criticism, and feelings of isolation.

Self-compassion also makes the possibility of failure less frightening, as failure is not an individual experience but a shared one—we all fail sometimes. This recognition provides an effective antidote to the fear, anxiety, and avoidance that commonly accompany self-criticism.

Facilitate self-compassion through mindful letter-writing:

Set aside 5 to 10 minutes to write a loving note to yourself on a separate piece of paper. Acknowledge and normalize your flaws, mistakes, and challenges. Point out the strengths you have drawn upon to move forward. Remind yourself that you will always have your own support and acceptance, and that you will always be in the company of others. Convey respect for your ability to tolerate difficult times and emotions.

USE THE WORDS BELOW TO WRITE A POEM, NOTE, OR PARAGRAPH

It

Voice

The

Very

Happy

Everybody

Thinking

About

With

Not

I'm

To

Acknowledging Resilience

When we ruminate about life's disappointments and our personal limitations, we risk overidentifying with them and becoming pessimistic.

With each setback, we gain resilience and growth. Recognizing this can help us transform discouragement into optimism.

What strengths have you drawn upon to work through a tough disappointment? What lessons or insights have you gained from it? How can you make use of this knowledge moving forward?

♡

When triggered, I have
the right to pause and take
my time to respond.

TIME TO REFLECT

Carve out routine time to reflect upon your life experiences.
By doing so, you might reveal surprising or useful insights.
Draw this scene's reflection in the water below.

Patchwork Apple

Fill in each square with discrete shapes, colors, lines, and textures.
Pay close attention to how you experience the making of each creation.

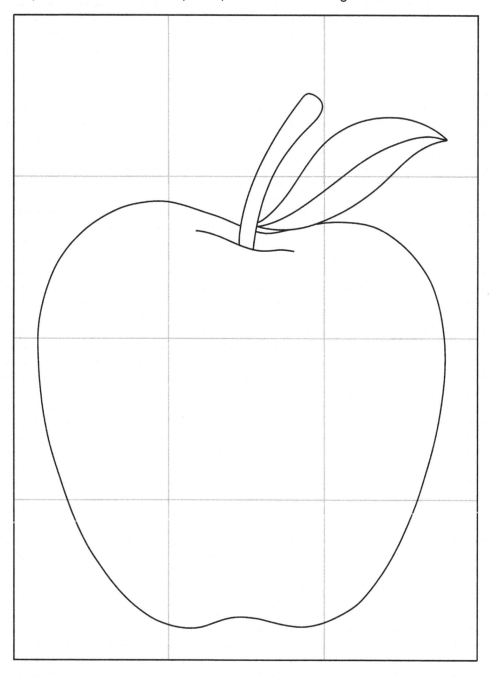

What Matters Most to You

The less of a discrepancy between one's personal value system and the way they spend their time, the more content the person. How closely does how you spend your time reflect what matters most to you?

_____

_____

_____

_____

_____

_____

_____

_____

_____

_____

_____

_____

_____

_____

_____

_____

_____

CREATING MOVEMENT

A moving body is often a happy one. Create movement by continuing the pattern below. First, add vertical wavy lines. Then, draw arched lines within the vertical segments.

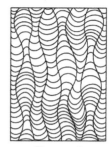

Example

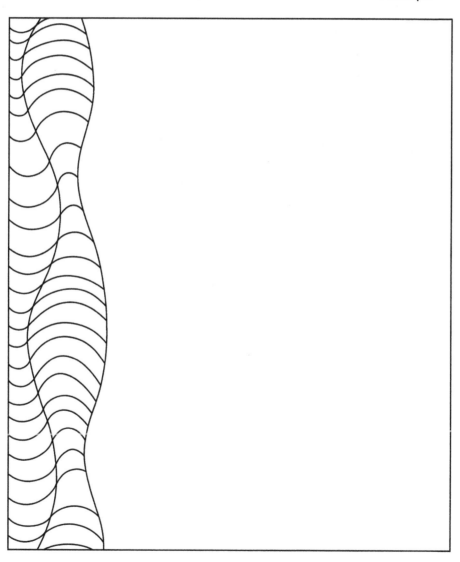

Letting Go of Secondary Pain

Chronic pain is common among those who suffer from depression. Fortunately, multiple studies demonstrate the benefits of mindfulness for pain reduction. If you try feeling simply curious and exploratory, you might be surprised to discover that your pain is different from how you normally experience it. So much of what we feel physically has to do with the meaning we attach to our sensations.

Begin by lying down or sitting in a private spot. With your eyes closed, gently take in and fully release several rounds of breath while scanning your body and letting go of any tension.

Draw your awareness to an area of discomfort. Focus on that spot and observe the sensations while continuing to breathe evenly and slowly. Become curious about your discomfort. How would you describe the feeling? Is it tight? Stabbing? Aching? Prickly? Observe whether it's stagnant or moving.

As you breathe calmly and evenly, note how capable you are of observing discomfort without responding to it.

The more frequently you do this exercise, the more substantial the benefits.

ALL ABOUT ME!

Add illustrations, doodles, and adjectives written in unique fonts to your *All About Me* page. Use the prompts provided for inspiration.

FAVORITES

FEARS

ALL ABOUT ME

PLACES

DREAMS

♡

No one is loved by everyone.
I am lovable even when
in the company of those
who cannot show me that.

Being vs. Doing

From a very young age, we are praised for active pursuits. The skill of *being*, on the other hand, is rarely cultivated or lauded. It sometimes feels wasteful to set aside time to just *be*. Ironically, setting aside a few minutes every day for mindfulness—honoring our time simply to be—has been thoroughly demonstrated to improve, not reduce, productivity.

What thoughts arise for you when you take time, or consider taking time, to practice mindfulness?

Soothing Depth Coloring

Take your time to color in the curves of the drawing below to help you reach or deepen a state of relaxation.

What You Nurture Will Grow

On the pots below, label each with a trait you would like to strengthen. Beneath the pots, list behaviors you can engage in to nurture each trait.

_____

_____

_____

_____

_____

_____

_____

_____

_____

_____

_____

_____

_____

Pacing through Life

We have all been told that moderation is key when it comes to certain life-style habits, but did you know that taking a moderate approach to *everything* contributes to greater life satisfaction? Take a look at your typical weekly routine, including recreation, work, socializing, exercise, and sleep. What are you doing too much or too little of?

PIXEL TREE

On the grid, draw a circle to represent the treetop. Draw branches within the circle, and a trunk that extends slightly outward from the circle to the bottom of the page. Color in the squares of the trunk, treetop, and background, making sure adjacent squares are different shades or colors.

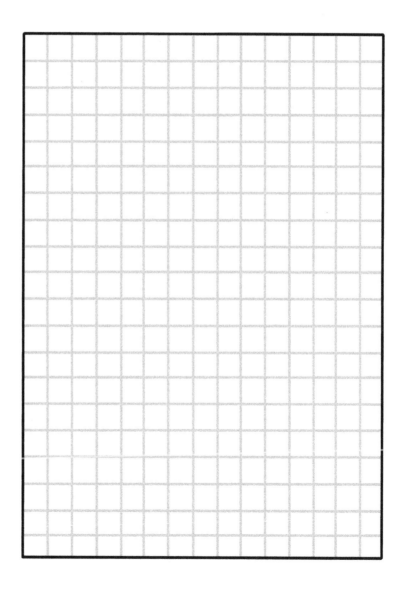

Example

Understanding and Releasing Anger

Anger is a common secondary emotion to more vulnerable emotions, like depression, self-doubt, and worry. Anger makes us feel strong and even motivated. Unfortunately, anger can also be irrational and push others away. Letting go of anger and getting in touch with softer, underlying emotions can help you find more adaptive ways of getting your needs met.

Close your eyes while in a comfortable seated or reclined position. Inhale deeply through your nose, hold your breath for three seconds, then exhale completely through your mouth. Continue with this pattern of breathing. Visualize oxygen entering your body and carbon dioxide leaving.

Direct your focus to your anger. See if you can identify its trigger, then ask yourself what underlying emotion anger is preventing you from experiencing. Perhaps it's fear, insecurity, or sadness.

Once you identify the underlying vulnerability, think about ways you might address it directly. Could you reveal it to someone else? Journal about it? Give yourself self-compassion and understanding?

HEALING BILATERAL, RHYTHMIC STROKE DRAWINGS

Bilateral drawing helps individuals work through painful experiences, allowing for improved mind-body integration and emotional regulation.

With a drawing utensil in each hand, close your eyes. Notice where you store emotional pain in your body. Draw your pain, using both hands. On top of your pain, use repetitive strokes for several minutes to push the pain away.

Being Seen

Satisfying relationships are ones in which we feel "seen" in the ways we see ourselves. Consider one of your closest relationships:

How are you seen in this relationship?

....

....

....

How do you see yourself?

....

....

....

How closely do you think your view of this person reflects their view of themself?

....

....

....

SETTING BOUNDARIES

Knowing when and how to effectively set boundaries with others is an essential component of self-care. Using the dots as guidelines, create an assortment of boundaries, or borders. Between the dots, list a few boundaries that you would like to work on. Use the remaining spaces to design and decorate boundaries as reminders of your intention to honor your limits.

Example

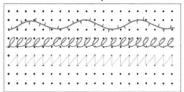

CITYSCAPE

Color the city buildings below. Add detail. Feel free to add typical and atypical features, and functional as well as decorative characteristics.

♡

*I see others fully and
connect with them through
my heart, not my head.*

Having Compassion for Your Intense Emotions

We learn early in life that certain emotions are "bad." The problem with this is that all emotions are a universal part of the human experience, and reacting to them with negativity compounds internal tension, shame, and negativity. When we instead approach unwanted emotions with curiosity and acceptance, they dissipate more quickly and surface less often.

What emotions are hardest for you to accept?

....

....

....

Where did you learn that these emotions were "bad"?

....

....

....

What are these emotions trying to communicate to you? How can you respond to them compassionately?

....

....

....

MUSIC AND CHEMISTRY

Music has the capacity to powerfully influence our moods. Make some simple drawings over the sheet music below, then color in your drawings, altering colors for each area created by the lines in the sheet music.

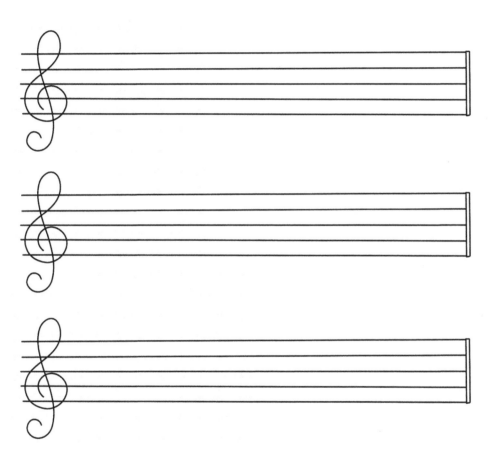

Example

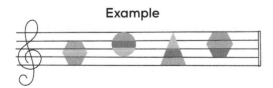

Reflective Listening and Mirroring

Giving our complete attention to others is not easy to master, but like building muscle, this strength can be developed with practice. As a result, you will notice that being present in relationships deepens acceptance, makes for more meaningful connections, and reduces feelings of isolation—for everyone involved.

Choose a day or week to dedicate yourself to being "other" oriented. Set your intention to hear what others say and repeat some of it back to them. Make sure to repeat a few of the very words you have heard, rather than making an interpretation of their meaning. Resist the urge to talk about something similar or change the subject.

To further your connection, make steady eye contact and nod your head to show you hear and understand. Vaguely mirror the other person's body positioning.

As you do this, take note of your experience of being fully present as well as how your presence is received.

LANDSCAPE ART

Fill in each of the layers of land with a unique line pattern. You might choose to use the same color for each layer, or distinguish layers by color.

Energizing Cat-Cow

Use this yoga pose first thing in the morning or anytime you need to release tension and boost energy.

Begin with palms and knees on the floor and a flat back, making a table shape. This exercise can also be done from a sitting position if needed.

As you inhale, roll your shoulders back and down along your spine while gently lifting your tailbone and head.

With an exhale, tuck your pelvis, lower your head, and arch like a frightened cat.

Repeat slowly for two minutes, fully taking in the sensations of each movement.

Next, keeping your knees and hands in the same spots, pull your right shoulder and right hip toward one another. Allow the rest of your body to stretch to the left. Now, draw the left shoulder and hip together, moving the opposite side of your body to the right.

Continue until you have released significant tension from the sides of your body.

LETTING GO

In the hot-air balloons below, write in self-defeating thoughts or beliefs that do not serve you. Color them in and imagine them floating away.

Rectangle Breath for Self-Soothing

Rectangle breath is a wonderful practice for bedtime or for when you're worrying or experiencing panic symptoms. It can be done sitting, or preferably, lying down.

Sit up straight or lie flat, with arms by your sides. Close your eyes.

Allow yourself to give in to gravity, feeling fully upheld by whatever is beneath you. Feel your limbs and head become heavier as you let go.

Turn your attention to your breath. Inhaling deeply, visualize your breath making its way up one entire side of your body, from foot to the top of your head. Hold your breath for a moment and imagine it traveling straight across your body to the other side. As you exhale, envision the breath moving down the length of your other side. To complete the rectangle, hold your breath for a moment, envisioning it making its way across your feet to its starting point.

See if you can complete 10 full cycles of rectangle breath.

Stained Glass Coloring
for Augmenting Compassion

As you color in the heart-covered stained glass window below, think of the many people, pets, and elements of the natural world that regularly bring you warmth and joy.

Random Acts of Kindness

Acts of kindness are true chemistry—they increase the body's levels of serotonin and dopamine, chemicals that generate feelings of happiness and contentedness. Routine and balanced displays of kindness are also positively associated with longevity and good health.

For one day, set your intention to committing five acts of kindness. Acts of kindness need not be major undertakings. They can be as simple as helping with a minor task, smiling at someone, or paying a compliment.

After you perform each act of kindness, bring your awareness to how you feel. Notice if you feel any spike in satisfaction, empowerment, joy, connection, or self-esteem. At the end of your day, assess your internal state again. Decide whether random acts of kindness are worth incorporating into your routine.

PERSPECTIVE IS EVERYTHING

Approaching a situation from a new angle can completely change your interpretation of it. As you color in the drawing below, consider whether it would be useful to shift your perspective on any situations you currently face, and how you can do so.

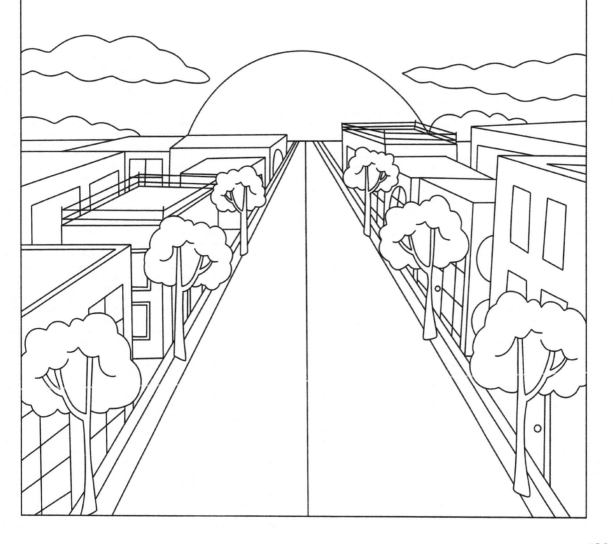

♡

*I fully experience each day,
knowing that my life is now,
not a future destination.*

Resources

Good Morning, I Love You: Mindfulness and Self-Compassion Practices to Rewire Your Brain for Calm, Clarity, and Joy by Shauna Shapiro, PhD. Scientifically explained mindfulness practices for attaining self-acceptance and fulfillment.

The Mindfulness Solution: Everyday Practices for Everyday Problems by Ronald D. Siegel, PsyD. Step-by-step approaches to achieving mindfulness for stress, anxiety, pain, and depression reduction.

Mindsight: The New Science of Personal Transformation by Daniel J. Siegel, MD. Rooted in interpersonal neurobiology, skills for changing the brain's circuitry for greater happiness, empathy, compassion, and resilience.

Start Here: Master the Lifelong Habit of Wellbeing by Eric Langshur and Nate Klemp, PhD. Training program for developing mindfulness, gratitude, and compassion.

WEBSITES

Behavioral Health Treatment Services Locator
FindTreatment.SAMHSA.gov

Imagine Mindfulness
ImagineMindfulness.com
Online donation-based stress reduction classes.

Inward Bound Mindfulness Education
IBME.com
Mindfulness programs for teens and adults.

Spirit Rock
SpiritRock.org
Meditation center offering online and in-person classes and trainings.

APPS
Aura
AuraHealth.io
Meditations, life coaching, music, hypnosis, and stories for emotional health.

Healthy Minds Program App
HMInnovations.org/meditation-app
Meditations and bite-size lessons for developing the skill of well-being.

COURSE
The Science of Well-Being by Laurie Santos
Coursera.org/learn/the-science-of-well-being
Offered by Yale University on Coursera. Overview of research on happiness, and practices for improving well-being and productivity.

References

American Psychiatric Association. *Diagnostic and Statistical Manual of Mental Disorders*. 5th ed. Washington, DC: American Psychiatric Publishing, 2013.

Baikie, Karen A., and Kay Wilhelm. "Emotional and Physical Health Benefits of Expressive Writing." *Advances in Psychiatric Treatment* 11, no. 5 (September 2005): 338–46. DOI.org/10.1192/apt.11.5.338.

Barrett, Bruce, Christine M. Harden, Roger L. Brown, Christopher L. Coe, and Michael R. Irwin. "Mindfulness Meditation and Exercise Both Improve Sleep Quality: Secondary Analysis of a Randomized Controlled Trial of Community Dwelling Adults." *Sleep Health* 6, no. 6 (December 2020): 804–813. DOI.org/10.1016/j.sleh.2020.04.003.

Capaldi, Colin A., Raelyne L. Dopko, and John M. Zelenski. "The Relationship between Nature Connectedness and Happiness: A Meta-analysis." *Frontiers in Psychology* 8 (September 2014). DOI.org/10.3389/fpsyg.2014.00976.

Carson, Shelley. "Creative Thinking and the Brain." *Harvard Health Publishing*. December 1, 2010. health.Harvard.edu/newsletter_article/creative-thinking-and-the-brain.

Congleton, Christina, Britta K. Hölzel, and Sara W. Lazar. "Mindfulness Can Literally Change Your Brain." *Harvard Business Review*. January 8, 2015. HBR.org/2015/01/mindfulness-can-literally-change-your-brain.

Fredrickson, Barbara L., Karen M. Grewen, Kimberly A. Coffey, Sara B. Algoe, Ann M. Firestine, Jesusa M. G. Arevalo, Jeffrey Ma, and Steven W. Cole. "A Functional Genomic Perspective on Human Well-being." *Proceedings of the National Academy of Sciences* 110, no. 33 (August 2013): 13684–13689. DOI.org/10.1073/pnas.1305419110.

Gara, Michael A., Robert L. Woolfolk, Bertram D. Cohen, Ruth B. Goldston, Lesley A. Allen, and James Novalany. "Perception of Self and Other in Major Depression." *Journal of Abnormal Psychology* 102, no. 1 (1993): 93–100. DOI.org/10.1037/0021-843X.102.1.93.

Kaimal, Girija, Hasan Ayaz, Joanna Herres, Rebekka Dieterich-Hartwell, Bindal Makwana, Donna H. Kaiser, and Jennifer A. Nasser. "Functional Near-infrared Spectroscopy Assessment of Reward Perception Based on Visual Self-expression: Coloring, Doodling, and Free Drawing." *The Arts in Psychotherapy* 55 (September 2017): 85–92. DOI.org/10.1016/j.aip.2017.05.004.

Killingsworth, Matthew. "The Future of Happiness Research." *Harvard Business Review* 90, no. 1–2 (January–February 2012): 88–89. PMID: 22299507.

Malchiodi, Cathy A. *Trauma and Expressive Arts Therapy: Brain, Body, and Imagination in the Healing Process.* New York: Guilford, 2020.

National Alliance on Mental Illness. "Depression." Accessed September 24, 2021. NAMI.org/About-Mental-Illness/Mental-Health-Conditions/Depression.

Robbins, Jim. "Ecopsychology: How Immersion in Nature Benefits Your Health." *Yale Environment 360.* January 9, 2020. e360.Yale.edu/features /ecopsychology-how-immersion-in-nature-benefits-your-health.

Siegle, Steve. "The Art of Kindness." Speaking of Health (blog). Mayo Clinic. May 29, 2020. MayoClinicHealthSystem.org/hometown-health/speaking -of-health/the-art-of-kindness.

Strauss, Clara, Kate Cavanagh, Annie Oliver, and Danelle Pettman. "Mindfulness-Based Interventions for People Diagnosed with a Current Episode of an Anxiety or Depressive Disorder: A Meta-Analysis of Randomised Controlled Trials." *PLoS One* 9, no. 4 (2014): e96110. DOI. org/10.1371/journal.pone.0096110.

Trivedi, Madhukar H. "The Link Between Depression and Physical Symptoms." *Prim Care Companion J Clin Psychiatry* 6, suppl. 1 (2004): 12–16. PMCID: PMC486942.

Van der Vennet, Renée, and Susan Serice. "Can Coloring Mandalas Reduce Anxiety? A Replication Study." *Journal of the American Art Therapy Association* 29, no. 2 (2012): 87–92. DOI.org/10.1080/07421656.2012.680047.

Zeidan, Fadel, Jennifer N. Baumgartner, and Robert C. Coghill. "The Neural Mechanisms of Mindfulness-based Pain Relief: A Functional Magnetic Resonance Imaging-based Review and Primer." *PAIN Reports* 4, no. 4 (August 2019): e759. DOI.org/10.1097/PR9.0000000000000759.

About the Author

 **Maggie C. Vaughan**, LMFT, PhD, is a licensed marriage and family therapist as well as a certified hypnotherapist and integrative mental health provider. For nearly 15 years, she has studied mind-body practices and incorporated them into her work. She offers therapy to adult individuals and couples in her private practice and is the founder of Happy Apple, a busy New York City psychotherapy center. Her insights have been featured by several media outlets, including *The New York Times*, *Huffington Post*, and BBC Radio. Dr. Vaughan lives in the New York City area with her family and can be found at EveryoneNeedsTherapy.com.

CPSIA information can be obtained
at www.ICGtesting.com
Printed in the USA
JSHW011936310322
24079JS00002B/2